CELEBRATING THE FAMILY NAME OF HERNÁNDEZ

Celebrating the Family Name of Hernández

Walter the Educator

SKB
Silent King Books
a WhichHead Entertainment Imprint

Copyright © 2024 by Walter the Educator

All rights reserved. No part of this book may be reproduced in any manner whatsoever without written permission except in the case of brief quotations embodied in critical articles and reviews.

First Printing, 2024

Disclaimer

This book is a literary work; the story is not about specific persons, locations, situations, and/or circumstances unless mentioned in a historical context. Any resemblance to real persons, locations, situations, and/or circumstances is coincidental. This book is for entertainment and informational purposes only. The author and publisher offer this information without warranties expressed or implied. No matter the grounds, neither the author nor the publisher will be accountable for any losses, injuries, or other damages caused by the reader's use of this book. The use of this book acknowledges an understanding and acceptance of this disclaimer.

Celebrating the Family Name of Hernández is a memory book that belongs to the Celebrating Family Name Book Series by Walter the Educator. Collect them all and more books at WaltertheEducator.com

USE THE EXTRA SPACE TO DOCUMENT YOUR FAMILY MEMORIES THROUGHOUT THE YEARS

HERNÁNDEZ

In the heart of ancient hills,

Celebrating the Family Name of

Hernández

Where whispers blend with time,

The name Hernández first unfurled,

A rhythm, a chime.

Carved in the winds of distant lands,

In valleys lush and green,

Hernández rose like morning light,

In every dawn unseen.

A name born of the earth's embrace,

Of fire, stone, and clay,

Hernández carried through the years,

Celebrating the Family Name of

Hernández

A melody in sway.

Through canyons deep and rivers wide,

Where eagles trace the sky,

Hernández spoke in voices strong,

Of futures drawing nigh.

In the forge where iron bends,

And sparks dance in the night,

Hernández shaped its destiny,

With hands both firm and light.

It's in the song of every leaf,

In the rustle of the trees,

Hernández dances with the wind,

In every tender breeze.

A lineage of strength and grace,

Celebrating the Family Name of

Hernández

Of honor held so high,

Hernández stands like ancient oak,

Beneath a boundless sky.

Through battles fought and won with pride,

In peace that follows strife,

Hernández echoes through the years,

In every pulse of life.

From the fields where crops arise,

To cities built with care,

Hernández walks with purpose clear,
Celebrating the Family Name of
Hernández

With courage, love, and flair.

In the laughter of a child's heart,

In the wisdom of the old,

Hernández weaves a tapestry,

With threads of silver and gold.

ABOUT THE CREATOR

Walter the Educator is one of the pseudonyms for Walter Anderson. Formally educated in Chemistry, Business, and Education, he is an educator, an author, a diverse entrepreneur, and he is the son of a disabled war veteran. "Walter the Educator" shares his time between educating and creating. He holds interests and owns several creative projects that entertain, enlighten, enhance, and educate, hoping to inspire and motivate you. Follow, find new works, and stay up to date with Walter the Educator™ at WaltertheEducator.com

Milton Keynes UK
Ingram Content Group UK Ltd.
UKHW022147190824
447134UK00016B/823